PUERTO RICO

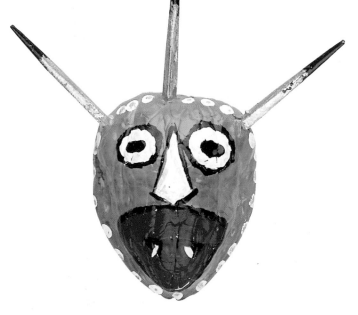

GROLIER
EDUCATIONAL

Published 1999 by Grolier Educational
Sherman Turnpike, Danbury, Connecticut.
Copyright © 1999 Times Editions Pte Ltd. Singapore.

Set ISBN: 0-7172-9324-6
Volume ISBN: 0-7172-9337-8

CIP information available from the Library of Congress or the publisher

Brown Partworks Ltd.

Series Editor: Tessa Paul
Series Designer: Joyce Mason
Crafts devised and created by Susan Moxley
Music arrangements by Harry Boteler
Photographs by Bruce Mackie
Subeditor: Roz Fischel
Production: Alex Mackenzie
Stylists: Joyce Mason and Tessa Paul

For this volume:
Designer: Barbara Borup
Writer: Dr. Aurea Rodriguez, Puerto Rican Institute for
the Development of Education
Editorial Assistants: Hannah Beardon and Paul Thompson

Printed in Italy

Adult supervision advised for all crafts and recipes,
particularly those involving sharp instruments and heat.

CONTENTS

PUERTO RICO:

Puerto Rico is a Caribbean island. On its west is the large island of Haiti and the Dominican Republic. To the east is an archipelago of islands, among them the Virgin Islands.

◀**San Juan** is one of the oldest cities in the New World. It is also a very charming city. In the old town houses are painted in a pleasing variety of colors. It is a banking center for its island neighbors and has some of the finest universities in the Caribbean. It attracts many tourists who enjoy the colonial architecture, the coastline, and the tropical climate.

Atlantic Ocean

Aricebec

SAN JUAN

Puerto Rico

Mayagüez

Cerro de Punta

Rio Grande de Manati

Ponce

Caribbean Sea

▲**The Madonna** plays a special role for the followers of the Roman Catholic Church. Puerto Rico is a Christian country, and most people belong to the Roman Catholic Church. Carved and painted religious figures, called *santos,* can be seen everywhere. These images are not only used in churches, but are kept in people's homes. Modern artists and craftsmen continue the traditions of earlier folk artists and still create these santos figures.

▲**El Morro** is part of the fortifications built by the Spanish in San Juan. These strong, tall buildings were meant to keep the English pirates away. The walls are 140 feet high and 20 feet thick. For a short period in the sixteenth century the English did control the fort. They did not come by sea but crept in from the land side of the structure. The fort is now a museum.

Virgin Islands

First Impressions

- **Population** 3,646,000
- **Largest city** San Juan with a population of 1,390,000
- **Longest river** Rio Grande de Manatí
- **Highest mountain** Mt. Punta at 4,389 ft.
- **Exports** Agricultural products
- **Capital city** San Juan
- **Political status** Commonwealth territory of the U.S.A.
- **Climate** Tropical
- **Art and culture** Wooden sculptures of saints. Salsa music is very popular, and the best musicians are Willie Colon and his band.

RELIGIONS

The Roman Catholic Church has been an important influence on life in Puerto Rico ever since the Spanish colonized the island in the fifteenth century. But the people never gave up their ancient gods, and today their form of Christianity is a little of both worlds.

THE PEOPLE OF Puerto Rico are a mix of three different racial and cultural groups: the Taínos, the original Puerto Rican islanders; the Spanish; and the Africans. By religion they are either Roman Catholics or Protestants.

Roman Catholicism was brought to the island by the Spanish *conquistadors,* or "soldiers," in 1493. The Catholics celebrate lots of festivals throughout the year. Every single town has its own patron saint. Special Catholic festivals include: *Fiestas de Cruz,* or Festival of the Cross; *Rosarios Cantados,* or Chanting the Rosary; and *villancicos* and *aguinaldos,* or Christmas Carols. The Catholics go to Mass at church every Sunday.

Some people have now converted to the Protestant faith. Many churches

have been built to provide places of worship for them.

Spiritualism was the "religion" of the Taínos before the Spanish came. They banned it but many Catholics still believe that the spirits of the dead wander the island at night.

Long ago everybody would leave out food at night in case the spirits got hungry. Even today in most houses plastic fruit can be seen on top of the refrigerator as an echo of the custom. Country folk are still very superstitious.

Santería, a form of spiritualism that was brought to Puerto Rico by African slaves, is also still practiced on the island. Some people combine the two different traditions and worship Roman Catholic saints as if they were spiritual gods. This form of worship is called the Cult of the Saints.

GREETINGS FROM **PUERTO RICO!**

Puerto Rico is a small island in the Caribbean Sea. It has a population of 3.2 million. The people of Puerto Rico speak Spanish and they also speak English as a second language.

The island became a colony of Spain in 1493 when the great explorer Christopher Columbus arrived at its shore. In 1898 the United States invaded the island, and a war treaty signed by Spain gave the island of Puerto Rico to the United States. The culture and traditions of the Puerto Ricans are a mixture of three different cultures: the Taíno, or original islanders; the Spanish; and the African.

How do you say...

Hello

¡Hola!

How are you?

¿Como estás?

My name is ...

Me llamo ...

Goodbye

Adiós

Thank you

Gracias

Peace

La paz

SAN JUAN BAUTISTA

San Juan Bautista, *or Saint John the Baptist, is symbolized by a lamb holding a cross. He is a much-loved saint, and his festival is a joyful, family celebration.*

San Juan Bautista, or "Saint John the Baptist," is the patron saint of San Juan, the capital city of Puerto Rico. His feast day is held on June 24 each year.

It was John who baptized Jesus in the River Jordan. This means that symbolically he washed away sin by dipping Jesus in the waters of the River Jordan. However, John knew that Jesus Christ was the Son of God and so did not need to be cleansed. John was a very holy man whose head was cut off when he angered the Roman governor ruling the land where he lived.

This saint has a special place in the hearts of Roman Catholics. His feast day is full of rituals and superstitions that bring people hope or make them feel happier about their lives.

His festival is both a family day and a national day. On the eve of Saint John's Day the city of San Juan prepares for the spiritual arrival of their patron saint. The faithful make offerings to the saint in the hope that he will bless them with fortune. They ask him for luck in love and to give them some knowledge about their future.

Thousands of people gather on the beaches. Families go

The churches are filled with ornate imagery and crosses. Masses are said for John the Baptist on his day.

The city of San Juan is supposed to be a place of miracles, and believers hope for something wonderful to happen on Saint John's Day. It is a family day. People go out for meals or gather at home. The food is spicy. A popular sauce is the sofrido, *made of coriander, sweet red chile peppers, tomatoes, onions, and garlic. This is eaten with stewed meat or chicken, rice, and beans. Olive oil is also used regularly in the island food.*

very early to find a good spot. At midnight everybody rushes into the water, recalling the baptism in the River Jordan. Some people dive backward nine times. They believe this act will bring them luck.

Many people prepare three cloves of garlic. They peel half of one, all of another, and the third is kept unpeeled. They place all three under their pillows. In the morning, on the day of the festival, each person closes their eyes and then chooses one clove from under the pillow. Picking the unpeeled clove brings good luck.

Another custom involves breaking an egg in a vase of water. The vase is left under the bed. On the next morning the contents are examined and the future read in the shapes of the egg white and yolk.

Families enjoy festive meals together. Rice and beans are served in spicy sauces.

MAKE A FISH BASKET

Use a fish design to decorate this pretty basket and to capture the flavor of the island of Puerto Rico.

Puerto Ricans love fish. One of their favorites is *bacalao*, a dried, salted codfish that is actually imported from the United States and eaten during the season of Lent. But Puerto Rico is an island, and there are many local fish to catch, including red snapper, octopus, sea bass, lobster, and crab.

YOU WILL NEED
24" x 24" sheet of paper with a different color on each side
Black marker pen
Scissors
Stapler

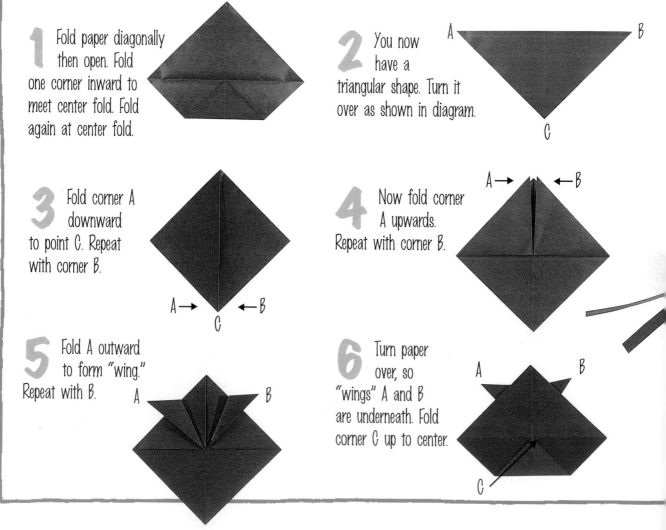

1 Fold paper diagonally then open. Fold one corner inward to meet center fold. Fold again at center fold.

2 You now have a triangular shape. Turn it over as shown in diagram.

3 Fold corner A downward to point C. Repeat with corner B.

4 Now fold corner A upwards. Repeat with corner B.

5 Fold A outward to form "wing." Repeat with B.

6 Turn paper over, so "wings" A and B are underneath. Fold corner C up to center.

7 Turn paper over. Fold lower section in half to meet upper section.

A   B

C

8 Fold again, so that C lies between wings A and B.

C

A   B

9 Turn over. Push E and F inward to make a square. Turn so that model makes a basket shape.

E

B

A

F

10 Fold top corners down. Decorate basket with black pen. Cut a strip of paper, about 14" long, fold in half down its length, then staple to folded corners to form a handle.

11 Snip the ends of a length of paper to make a tail. Staple to basket as shown. Fill your fish basket with candy and you have a fine gift for friends and family.

11

SANTIAGO APOSTOL

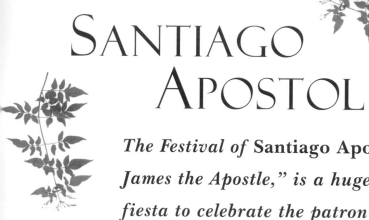

The Festival of Santiago Apostol, "Saint James the Apostle," is a huge and important fiesta to celebrate the patron saint of Spain.

The Festival of *Santiago Apostol* is the most famous fiesta in Puerto Rico. It honors Saint James, patron saint of Spain, and is held in the town of Loiza Aldea.

The festival is celebrated for three days from July 25. Each of the three days honors three different aspects of the saint: *Santiago de los Hombres,* "Saint of Men"; then *Santiago de las Mujeres,* "Saint of Women," and lastly, *Santiago de los Niños,* "Saint of Children."

The saint has three statues. Every year three homes look after one each of the statues. It is thought a great honor to be chosen as the *mantenedora,* or "keeper," of one of the statues.

The festival is held so that people can show their gratitude to Saint James for all his good deeds. On his day people give money to buy candles and ribbons to decorate his shrine. Parades and processions celebrate his holy life.

The elders and young women of the town plan the festivities. Preparation begins weeks before. Early on the morning of July 1 church bells ring and band music is played to tell the town that it is time to start work for the festival of Saint

James. Women start making costumes and dresses, masks, candles, and candies.

The masks are made of coconut shells or cardboard. They are very similar to the masks of the Yorubas, West Africans who were brought to the island as slaves by the Spanish *conquistadors*, or "soldiers," in the sixteenth century. The parade shows how the African and Spanish cultures have formed Puerto Rico.

On July 25 the celebration begins with a Mass in honor of the three Santiagos. The town plaza is colorfully decorated. Small red, yellow, and blue flags are also put up.

A VISION OF THE PAST

In 1493 the island was colonized by the Spanish, who brought their Christian faith, their music, and their food. Africans, who arrived as slaves, also added their traditions to the island. These two influences blended with the native culture. During most island parades the citizens proudly display their ethnic traditions and dress up in historical costumes. The Spanish dancer and the old time fruitseller are popular folk costumes.

Everyone in the town goes to Mass. Afterward the procession starts. The statue of Santiago of the Men is carried by men specially chosen for the event. The statue is heavy so they take turns in carrying it on their shoulders.

Men wearing costumes and masks join with the procession behind the statue. *Caballeros,* or "horseriders," trot alongside the statue to guard it against evil. They are dressed in brilliant shining colors as medieval Spanish knights. Their masks are made of painted wires. The hats are decorated with ribbons of many colors and lots of *cascabeles,* or "bells."

They are followed by strangely dressed groups of men known as the *vejigantes, los viejos,* and the *locas.*

The vejigantes wear grotesque masks with three big horns to represent evil. They wear large dresses with wide sleeves colored red, black, blue, and gray.

Los viejos, or the "old men," dress in rags. Their masks are made from shoeboxes, bags, and cardboard. They play music called the *bomba y plena,* which is based on African music.

The most strangely dressed group is the locas. They are men who are dressed as "crazy" women with blackened faces. They go through the town with brooms and vases, sweeping and cleaning the streets and the balconies of houses. In return people give them money.

The locas are not allowed to go into the church. They must wait outside and then join the procession as it moves through the

The highly colorful masks look as scary as possible. The devil faces are designed to frighten bad people and make them behave well!

Finally, the procession ends at the place where a vision of Santiago de los Niños was once seen.

The parade is by now crowded and loud with music. It halts for a while for a grand *carreras* or horserace, to begin. The *caballeros* ask the mantenedora for the honor of riding with the flag of the saint. The locas, the viejos, and the vejigantes all dance and play jokes on the crowds.

The next day a procession is held to honor Santiago de las Mujeres. The following day a third procession is held for Santiago de los Niños. The festival takes a whole a week, and everybody enjoys dance parties and lots of festive food.

town to a place where the Santiago de los Niños performed a miracle.

When the statue of the Santiago de los Hombres passes the house in which the Santiago de las Mujeres statue is kept, the latter is brought out into the street to salute Santiago de los Hombres. The men carrying it bow three times. Then the other statue leaves its house and joins the procession. This ritual is performed again at the house that is taking care of the third statue, Santiago de los Niños.

SAINT JAMES

There are many stories about Saint James. There is a shrine to him in Spain, and there is a fascinating story that explains this holy site.

IN A LOVELY TOWN in Spain there lived a lonely young man. He was in Santiago de Compostela studying to be a knight. He was very young, and he had left his home, his mother, his sisters, and his brothers far away in the country.

He knew it was a good, brave thing to be a knight. He longed to serve his king and defend his country. However, the boy was young and lonely.

Often he prayed to the Virgin Mary to let him see his own mother again or asked God to help him be a happier, braver knight. He tried hard not to be unhappy. One day, however, he felt he was unable to put on a cheerful smile for the other young knights.

The young knight called for his favorite horse. As he saddled the horse, he murmured in the animal's ear. He told him that they were going to have a quiet ride along the seashore. Today neither of them was going to work.

The knight knelt down in the stable and prayed to the Virgin and all the saints to help him be a better person. He wanted a sign, he told them, a sign to let him know his life was going to be better and he was going to be a brave and good knight.

It was a bright, sunny day. The knight and his horse galloped happily over the fields, through some woods, and then they saw the sparkling waters

of the sea. They raced to the cliff's edge and trotted along, taking in the salt air.

The knight grew dreamy and thought about his mother and his home. This made him sad again. So he started to pray once more, asking that this sadness be taken from him.

However, the horse was happy to be outside. It made little hops and skips as it trotted on the cliff's edge. Then a strange shadow showed in the water. The horse stopped in alarm. The knight was puzzled. Suddenly, a great, marble ship lifted from the waves. Its smooth sides were covered by seaweed and small, green sea creatures. It did not look like any ordinary boat. The horse leaped up and whinnied in fear.

The animal was so frightened that it stumbled. The knight and his horse plunged over the cliff and fell into the deep, deep sea.

They did not drown. A miracle saved them. The knight landed, not in the sea, but on the ship itself. His horse was held carefully by the waves while the ship rose in splendor from the waters. The knight's cloak was covered in shells. A gentle wind pushed the boat, the knight, and the horse to shore.

It was the boat that had carried the body of Saint James. It had been pushed from the shores of distant Palestine and had come all the way to Spain. There is a shrine now to Saint James in Compostela. The knight went on to lead a brave, happy life.

MAKE AN ANIMAL MASK

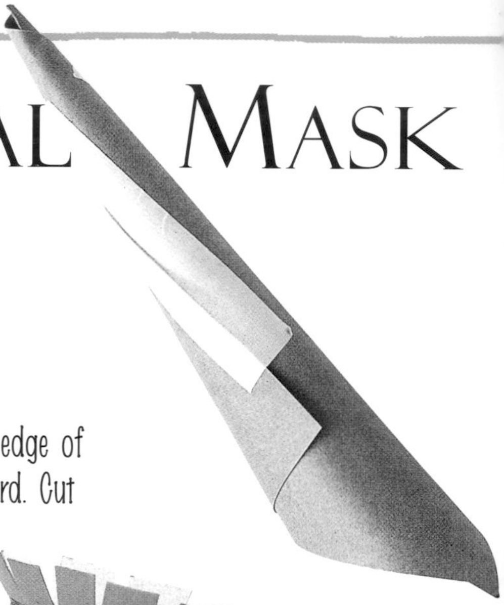

Animal masks are hugely popular at Puerto Rican festivals. They are part of a tradition brought by the African slaves who were transported to Puerto Rico by the Spanish.

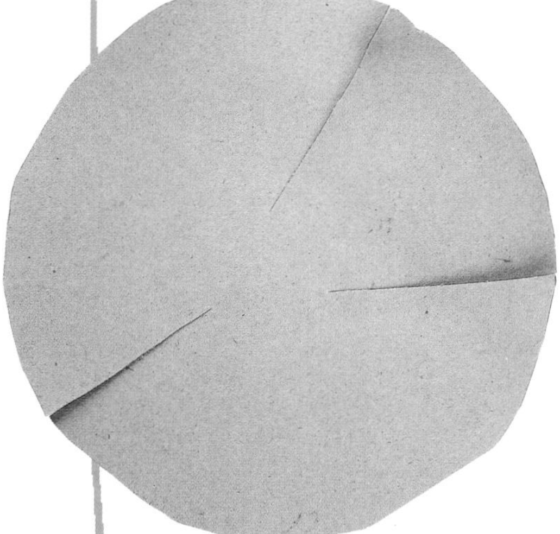

1 For the face, draw around edge of dinner plate laid on cardboard. Cut the circle out. Cut three slits in circle. To form shallow conical shapes, make a dart at each slit, fixing with tape. For the snout, make a cardboard cylinder 3" in radius. Tape edges together. Cut a mouth. Tape cardboard strips with jagged tooth shapes to sides of mouth.

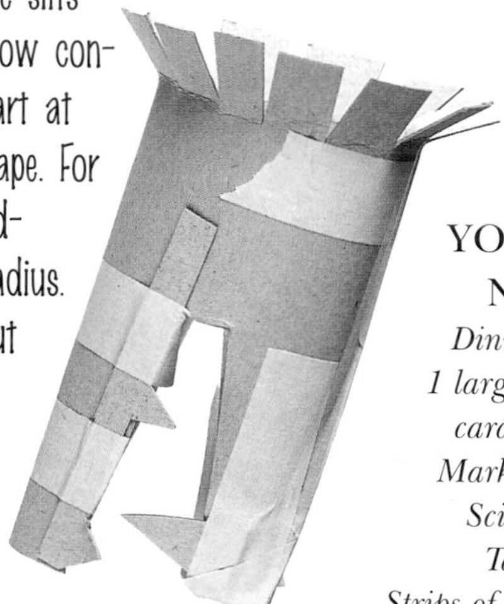

YOU WILL NEED

Dinner plate
1 large piece of cardboard
Marker pen
Scissors
Tape
Strips of newspaper
Glue
Paintbrush
Can of white wall paint
Poster paints

2 Snip the other end of the snout. For the horns, roll cardboard cones about 6" in length. Fix with tape. Snip the wide base and flatten snipped edges to face. Fix with tape. Cut eyes into the face.

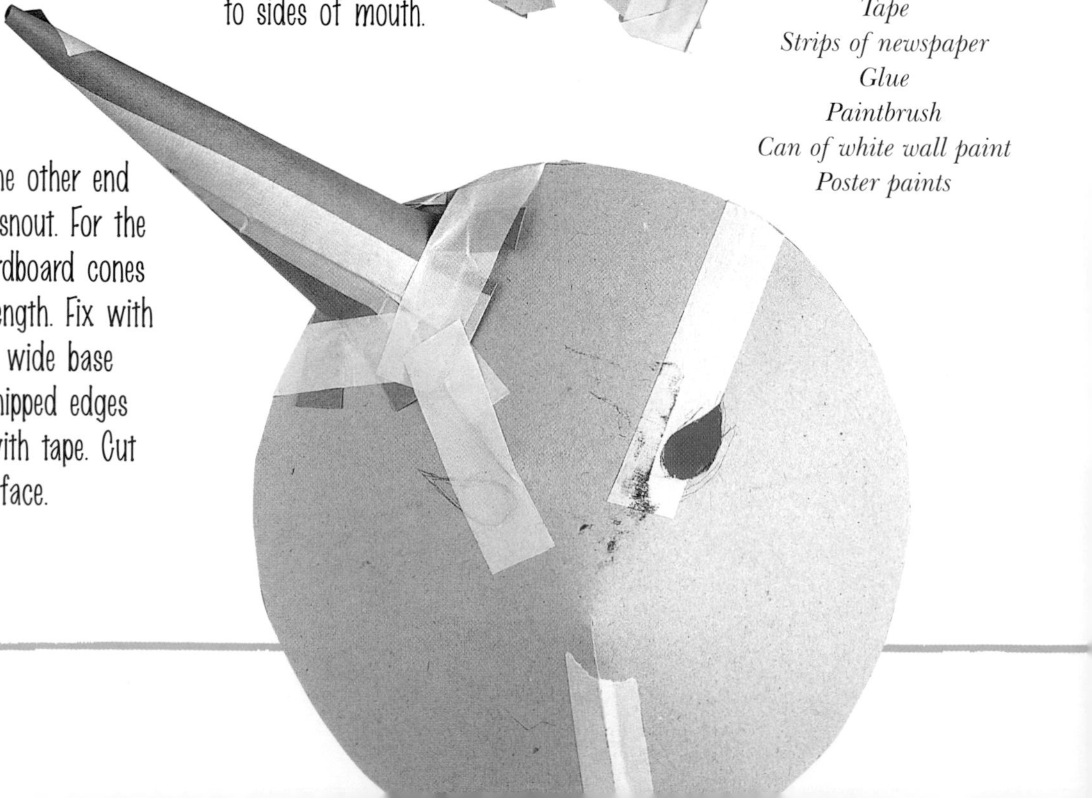

3 Flatten snipped edges of snout against face. Fix with tape. Layer strips of newspaper over entire mask. applying glue between each layer. Allow to dry. Apply a smooth coat of white wall paint over entire mask. Allow to dry.

4 Color with poster paints to create a bright and strange beast face. When paint is dry, varnish if you wish. The mask can be hung on the wall, or you may tape elastic across the back to hold mask over your face.

CARNIVAL

Carnival has grown from a religious feast to a grand fiesta of dance and costume. People dress in funny clothes or wear masks that recall their heritage.

Carnival is an old tradition in the Roman Catholic Christian world. It takes place on the eve of a 40-day fast called "Lent." In olden days, to prepare for Lent, everyone used up the foods that would not last, such as butter and cream. They also prepared for the fast with an enormous meal.

This feast became a party, then a carnival lasting for the week before Lent began. The Spanish Catholics who colonized South America brought this fiesta with them.

Carnival happens in February. Every town in Puerto Rico organizes parades and ceremonies. Groups of people join together to prepare floats, masks, costumes, and music for the parades that go through every *plaza,* or "square," and street.

Each town selects a Carnival Queen, and a costume ball is held to crown the queen of the carnival. The queen is chosen by those who organize the carnival activities. The queen then presides over the carnival parade.

The island is famous for its rum drinks. These are served in festive style during carnival time. The coqui is the famous "green frog" of Puerto Rico. People in the parade dress up as coquis. Many women wear folk costumes with large, swirling skirts.

The largest Lenten carnival in South America is the *Mardi Gras* in Rio de Janeiro, Brazil. However, even the smallest towns in Puerto Rico take pride in putting on a grand display for Carnival.

The costumes are lavish. Some may be playful clown figures, while others imitate religious or historical figures. Prizes are given to the best and most beautiful *comparsa*, or "parade float." On the last day crowds gather in the town square to dance, play jokes, and have fun.

LOS INOCENTES

The Christmas season celebrates not only the birth of Christ but also other events that happened around the time of His birth. Los Inocentes *recalls the Baby Jesus's escape from a cruel, tragic act by King Herod.*

Two days after Christmas is the fiesta *Dia de los Inocentes,* the "Day of the Innocents." There is a big celebration in the town of Hatillo on December 28.

The Day of the Innocents recalls the cruelty of King Herod. He ruled the land where Joseph and Mary, the parents of Jesus, lived. Herod heard rumors that a king was born, so he ordered all baby boys to be killed. An angel warned Joseph, and the family escaped from Herod's soldiers. Los Inocentes is held in memory of all the babies who died in the purge.

People prepare floats for the parade. Men dress up in elaborate costumes and masks, and it is hard to recognize any of them under their disguise. The men represent King Herod's soldiers who, house by house, killed the boys.

Little boys in Puerto Rico dress in white and go around Hatillo asking people for money or candy. They take care to hide

Cars are covered in flowers, and musicians dress up for the parade. Hats and dresses in patriotic stars and stripes are worn.

22

from the masked men because, if the men see a little boy, they will "kidnap" him and take him away to the floats. The parents of the "kidnapped" boy have to call and look for their son in every float before the boy is given back to them. People have lots of fun doing this. They play tricks on their friends and tell silly stories to fool each other.

Another tradition on this day is for the men to try to climb up a greased pole. This game also causes much fun and laughter.

Go to see the little horses, Look how they run. Go to see the little horses, Look how they run down the roads. Little one, Come, come, come, sit down here, The little horses run like this, like this, like this.

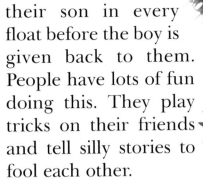

VAMOS A LOS CABALLITOS

Va-mos a los ca-ba-lli-tos Mi-ra co-mo co-rren u-na ca-

rre-ra Cin-co cen-ta-vos Ven, ven, ven, si-én-ta-te a-

quí Los ca-ba-lli-tos co-rren a-sí, a-sí, a-sí.

KING HEROD

This is the story of how Baby Jesus was sent by God to save the people of Judea, and how God helped Joseph save Jesus from King Herod.

A LONG TIME AGO, in Bethlehem in the land of Judea, Jesus Christ, the Son of God, was born. His mother was the Virgin Mary, her husband was Joseph.

That night some shepherds tending their sheep in the fields near Bethlehem saw a large white star in the sky. There was music, and an angel's voice told the shepherds not to be afraid because God had sent His Son, Jesus, to save the people of Judea from evil.

When the shepherds followed the star, it led them to a humble stable in Bethlehem. Here lay the Baby Jesus, watched over by Mary and Joseph and the animals in the stable. The shepherds knelt in deep respect.

Meanwhile, in a faraway land called Palestine, three wise men who studied the planets had also seen the great star.

They knew it was special, and as the news spread that a new king had been born, they followed the star to Bethlehem in Judea.

When the wise men arrived, they visited the ruler of Judea, King Herod. He was a harsh and powerful king, and he became worried when he heard that the wise men wanted to visit the new king. He did not want the people to have their own king, and he wanted his own son to rule after his death.

Herod pretended to the wise men that he too wanted to go and worship the new king. He asked them to find Jesus and report back to him. Secretly, however, he planned to kill the child.

The three wise men continued their journey. They followed the star until it stopped over the place where Jesus lay.

When they saw Jesus, they fell on their knees and worshiped him.

That night all three wise men had the same strange dream. In the dream they were told not to tell King Herod where Jesus could be found. So instead of reporting back to the king, they went home to Palestine along a different road.

When King Herod found out what had happened, he was angry. How could he find the child now? Then he had an idea. He had recently made all the people of Judea write down where they lived and who was in their families. This was called a census. So he knew where all the baby boys in his land were living. He sent soldiers to kill all the infants. In this way he thought he would also kill Jesus. This terrible crime came to be called the "Massacre of the Innocents."

That night God appeared to Joseph and told him he must flee with his child to a country called Egypt. Joseph did as he was told, and Jesus was saved from the wicked king.

When King Herod died, God again appeared to Joseph and told him he could return home. At last Jesus could grow up in peace, destined to go out in the world to spread the word of God.

LAS NAVIDADES

Las Navidades *means "the birthday." It is Christmas, the birth of Christ, and this date is celebrated over several weeks. Many local customs show both Spanish and African cultural heritage, but some show newer influences.*

Christmas, or *Las Navidades,* is celebrated by all in Puerto Rico. It is the longest and most exciting celebration of the year. It begins at the end of November and ends in January. After Christmas there is Three Kings Day, on January 6. This holiday is special to children, because this is the time when, at last, they are given their Christmas presents.

After Three Kings Day Puerto Ricans celebrate for another eight days. These are called the *octavitas,* or "little eights." Many people use the octavitas to take a vacation and visit their relatives in the countryside.

The Christmas season shows the influence of the United States. This is the newest element to be added to the cultural mix of Puerto Rico. People put colored lights up all over their houses and hang lights in the streets so that the whole town is lit

Images of Mary and the Baby Jesus can be found in most Roman Catholic churches. At Christmas they are surrounded by model animals and visitors. It is a seasonal custom for people to form musical groups called parrandas. *They play traditional instruments such as the* cuatro *(right), a type of mandolin.*

up. Santa Claus and his reindeer are now also a popular part of the Christmas season.

The Puerto Ricans make very beautiful creches, or nativity scenes. These are models of the stable where the Baby Jesus was born. Stores decorate their windows with lovely statuettes and images of the Virgin, the Baby, the stable animals and shepherds, and the "three wise men."

Another old tradition that may have come from Africa is called the *parranda*. Small groups of people get together with musical instruments. They visit friends and sing traditional songs to them. The music and singing are noisy. Then the whole party moves onto another house. The evening goes on with more and more people and louder and louder music. Friends may even be woken in the middle of the night!

On Christmas Eve, or *Nochebuena*, families enjoy a meal of roast pork before going to Midnight Mass. Some churches recall the birth of Christ with live animals and with children dressed as Mary, Joseph, the shepherds, and the "three wise men."

COFFEE

Puerto Rican coffee, especially from the area called Yauco, once had a reputation for being the best in the world. The island has the right environment in which to grow the plant that yields the coffee bean, yet this plant never grew there until it was introduced by the Spanish colonists. They brought slaves from West Africa to work on the coffee plantations. Coffee is one of the many foods the Spanish brought to the island that are now part of the local diet.

LOS REYES MAGOS

Los Reyes Magos *are the three wise men who followed a star. It led them to a stable and the Baby Jesus. This festival is devoted to children.*

The three wise men of this Bible story are also known as the three kings, or the magi. They lived in a country called Palestine, and they were knowledgeable. They knew that a sign from the sky meant that something unusual would happen on Earth. They followed a bright star, and it took them to see the Baby Jesus, Son of God.

There is a festival for the three kings that is held on January 6. The celebration is a custom of the Roman Catholic and Eastern Orthodox branches of the Christian Church.

On the evening of January 5, the day before Three Kings Day, Puerto Rican children look for cardboard boxes that their parents have hidden around the house. These can be of any

The night before Three Kings Day children place little boxes of grass under their beds and watch for the star that will guide the kings to their homes.

FRIED PLANTAINS

Peel the plantains as you would a banana. Cut them on the diagonal into large oval slices about ¼" thick.

Heat half the oil in a large frying pan over medium high heat. Add half the plantains so that they fit in one layer in the pan. Cook on one side for three minutes until soft and golden. Turn with a spatula. Cook on the other side for three minutes until soft and golden.

Remove the cooked slices and transfer to a plate under a grill on low heat. Then cook the rest of the plantain slices in batches.

Serve as a vegetable side dish with a main meal.

SERVES FOUR
3 large, ripe plantains
2 oz. cooking oil

size. When they find them, they fill them with green grass to feed the camels on which the three kings will arrive. They leave candy and water for the three kings. They also put a letter in the box asking the kings to leave a gift. The boxes are then put under their beds. Adults also exchange gifts.

In San Juan there is a great procession on this day, and free gifts of toys and candy are given to the city's children. Families often go to the country to visit grandparents and other relatives, where they enjoy a festive meal, make music, sing, and also recite the rosary, or prayer beads, together.

In the countryside families even greet strangers as they pass, and sometimes these unknown guests are invited in to sing and eat. This friendly time lasts for eight days, known as the *octavitas,* or the "little eights."

PATRON SAINT DAY

Every town in Puerto Rico has a patron saint. Celebrations begin 10 days before the feast day, so there is always a party somewhere!

The patron saint festivals, or *fiestas patronales*, are celebrated all over Puerto Rico at different times of the year. Each town has its own patron saint with his or her own saint's day.

Saints are an important part of the hopes and beliefs of Roman Catholics. They believe the saints talk to God on behalf of the faithful.

The traditional fiestas patronales, called *Fiestas de Cruz*, are held in May. An altar with flowers and nine steps is built, and a cross is moved up a step each day until the end of the feast. *Rosario cantados*, religious songs, are sung to the rosary throughout.

WORDS TO KNOW

Altar: A table on which worshippers leave offerings, burn incense, or perform ceremonies.

Baptize: A ritual to mark entry into the Christian faith. It involves dipping into or being marked by water.

Census: A count of all the people in a country, region, or area.

Colony: A land that is ruled by people from another country.

Conquistadors: The Spanish soldiers who conquered South and Central America in the sixteenth century.

Fast: To go without some or all kinds of food and drink deliberately.

Feast day: A day on which a religious event or the life of a saint is celebrated.

Lent: The 40 days between Ash Wednesday and Easter.

Mass: A Christian ritual in which bread and wine are used to commemorate the Last Supper of Jesus Christ.

Medieval: To do with the Middle Ages, the period between the fifth and the fifteenth centuries.

Patron saint: A saint who is special to a particular group. Nations, towns, and professions have patron saints.

Protestant: A member of one of the Protestant churches, which together form one of the main branches of Christianity. The Protestants split from the Roman Catholic Church in the sixteenth century.

Roman Catholic: A member of the Roman Catholic Church, the largest branch of Christianity. The head of this church is the pope.

Rosary: A set of prayers or the string of beads that people use to keep count of them. There is one bead for each prayer.

Saint: A title given to very holy people by some Christian churches. Saints are important in the Roman Catholic Church.

Shrine: A place that is sacred to the memory of a holy person.

ACKNOWLEDGMENTS

WITH THANKS TO:

Dr. Aurea Rodriguez.
Vale Antiques, London.
Mary Walker, London.

PHOTOGRAPHY:

All photographs by Bruce Mackie and White Backgrounds except: John Elliott p. 28.
Cover photograph by Katie Vandyk.

ILLUSTRATIONS BY:

Fiona Saunders pp. 4 – 5. Tracy Rich p. 7. Robert Shadbolt p. 17. Maps by John Woolford.

Recipes: Ellen Dupont.

Set Contents